Wave Books Seattle/New York

Anthony McCann

Published by Wave Books

www.wavepoetry.com

Copyright © 2014 by Anthony McCann

Wave Books titles are distributed to the trade by
Consortium Book Sales and Distribution
Phone: 800-283-3572 / SAN 631-760X

Library of Congress Cataloging-in-Publication Data
McCann, Anthony.
[Poems. Selections]
Thing music / Anthony McCann. — First Edition.
pages cm
ISBN 978-1-933517-97-1
ISBN 978-1-933517-96-4 (trade pbk.)
I. Title.
PS3613.C3453A6 2014
811'.6—dc23
2013046735

Designed and composed by Quemadura
Printed in the United States of America

9 8 7 6 5 4 3 2 1

First Edition

Wave Books 045

In the slick of the thing music   JACK SPICER

near your dumb bank.   JOHN ASHBERY

THING MUSIC

THING MUSIC

THE DAY

In this coupling
　　of speech
　　where everything
begins　　where
shimmering
began
　　please

put on my voice

and through
　　this voice

my eyes

　　　I mean

this ringing
　　in my eyes

on the day
it went away

I mean   the Day
it goes away

It is
the always
dying sound

the glimmer
of the bell

and the trees
ringing with light

Would you

touch
    these breeding
nouns

these wires
are alive

in the silent
hiss
    of space

as slipping
its face turns

rotates
in the leaves

the clarity
and shade

I want to say
Today

but today
it is *the Day*

that entered
in *my* face

I went there
on a sound

was smeared

with little shapes

while air
tumbled
through the chairs

  silent
clothes

  and bones

This doorway
looks
unsaid
as the animal

   descends   It opened

     up its
       flesh
   and landed
  in the day

the furling
   unfurled
world

cool
shadows
in each cleft

It's where
I come from   Where
I say

leaves
  twiddled

then

grew grave

MOUTH GUITAR

Lips
of
pulsing
loam

Blood
bubbles
blowing
speech

I cut off my head

and carried it

through the streets

The Dow was up
13 points   NASDAQ

is a bad move
in any poem
It courts

relevance   I carried

my head,
et cetera

by the hair,
et cetera

through the real streets
of the FANATICAL WOUND

THING MUSIC

I am not the word
You are not the word
I am not the thing
You are not the thing

We are the shadows
the names make
when they cross
the Bodylands

Table people
            Mirror people

We cross the thing-like land

While the bees
drool in the flowers
the sun
drools on the bees

And the Strangeness of my body   And the
Strangeness of your body

You're pulling ribbons from your throat
to grace the thing-like land

We grace the thing-like land
with breaths
replacing
feats

With breaths
replacing feet

But the land
inside the land
still stutters there unsaid

We   pause
to face
these trees

Leaves
stammer
on their twigs

When I find my real body (dead)
        I proclaim my living body (dead)

So blue it *is* a word

        Light stammers on our eyes

when we find it by the rocks
dead and real as the sky

SPEAKER

Behind
the scrolling face

there is

a real skull
and in the skull

a word
and sometimes

in that word
there is

a little throat

while around us
scream the hands
in the happy
Social Room

Please notice
Little Hands

say
the Little Hands

when I reached back
and whacked a man
in that inadvertent room

But I think
it is
to wiggle
that the Word
was
given rooms—

rooms so full of hands
and planted
eyes
in skulls

It is
the Social Room
so full
of eyes and skulls—

where the speaker
closed her eyes

as if
there were a throat

We were sitting on the floor
We sat
and arched our throats

One sound
like another
conjured
other sounds

It was through the window then
that I saw
the Flower Tree
hand out
bleeding
throats
in the furthest
yellow light

Flower Tree
I say

For my voice
I gathered lips

I make a picture
with my face

but my throat
is not my own

LANDSCAPE FOR BRIAN EVENSON

I said *paint*
I smelled paint
when I lived
underground

Sky-colored paint
paint covered with worms

You are my father
I said to the worms

You are my mother

You are the hair
of my throat
tasting dirt

Having tasted dirt
the moon increased
Night is *right there*
I said to the worms

But when I went
aboveground
I saw things
I saw words

And having tasted the dirt
with my dirt
covered face

having crawled
with my feet
and tasted the roads

and been stabbed
once more
in the throat
by the words

I tasted
leaf   weather
salt   color
and worms

You are my father
you are my mother
you are my sister
I said to the words

And this fly
on my knuckle
is love in the world

I said
to the dirt
in the throat
of the words

LET THE RIGHT ONE IN

I. APPLE
BOBBING

To the party
through the dark
men hoisted
darkened tubs.
I could almost
hear the screaming
beside the
little fence.
But in the poem
Social Life
I failed and
turned away
flashing
tiny teeth,
little
teeth marks
in my face.
Above me:

spotlit trees
on something
like a hill
where I'd preside
in social life
inside the way
I'd turned away.
I mean:
this way
I turn
to see you
to lock
into your face—
it hurts
my
little face,
the face
in my
big face.
For when you
turn away
I fail
and when I fail,
I turn away.
It's as if
we'd

wanted something
but our little
feelers got ripped out.
I do think
we wanted something.
I stick my head back in my face

2 . PRIVATE LIFE

This was social life:
underwater with my head.
But in private life
I clapped
and licked
your little face.
Your face
grew
trebled
and enormous
and then you entered
in my face.
And we was darkened speech
through something
like the days.
But in the poem

Social Life

I disappeared into my face.
I put my face in buckets:
this made me flashing teeth.
I can faintly
hear the cheers
where I'm
underwater here.
I can hear the screaming here.
And then I turned away.

DEATH VALLEY
FOR NOELLE

Listen and you hear it coming.
It gives you land to be there—
a vast something, under a crag,
as peremptory as vision.

The desert floor
lurks and blinks;
it has this
Flicker Presence

called forth by the verbs
we just pinned to its bare face.

And the sea
singing overhead—
the sea
that isn't there.

Friend, in my brain
you are this hidden face.

The rest is light and distance,
invisible as land.

THE NOUNS

But I'm a plant
> you said

> bedewed
> in object drool

> Sometimes
>> I was shoes

>> I looked down
>> into the earth
> I saw

>> the feathered clouds

>> I saw
>> a rash of light:
>>> Heads 'n' Things,
>>>> *The Nouns*

>>> like when a head comes off
>> and light spreads across the room

There was a cloud of light
                next to a living hand
        I saw
                    the blank and silent dirt
            all afternoon   the land

and day: a square and rippled thing

we rode sounds
into its throat

leaves twitched
in the white wind

light entered
every hole

    Everything was noise
                the *Whole* distance
        All the land

Light poured
into the house
onto our bodies
behind glass

You gestured
toward the egg
and distance
in that room

that my body
might be pierced
at any moment
by the world

Thus I saw
your living head

your eyes
went up and down

Air rushed along the roof
There was a brand-new sound

CREDO (WIND)

Grass swooning
in the far
is the distance
in my chest,

near and
being flesh,
of place:
a lighter mouth.

Beneath
the wiggled leaves
light enters
in the meat.

It gives me
wiggled arms.
I believe
that I have arms.

Finally,
I believe it,
like a tongue
touches a lip—

the light's
a little whip, I say
and looked away
and walked.

Your face
was on the water.
I could not
hear the sounds

of pleasure
in the bee.
The wind
licks everything.

THE CITY

if I close my eyes and hear
    the city is right there
        this darkness pushing blood
    outside is only light

    I think I smell your rooms

and bright dishevelment of breeze

  when I'd open I'd see eyes
    green to tree to tree

    oh what is a town
        it's a sidewalk when we meet

afternoon   the place
  we become each other here

    light gives the world its grace
    socks bleeding in a ditch
   it's a gaze and it's a pit

nothing moved but leaves
and time on human things

as if underneath the boards
the moon sunk through the earth
to rooms of blinding glass
tangled in the roots

I could see a whole life there

lungs flapping in a cave

but I have not watched long enough
I should have watched all day

THE SHAPES

THE SHAPES

The sun through a window put a shape on your head
Another shape moved—on the pillows—the walls
Music and Light at the All Morning Motel
When you slam the car door the whole water vibrates

We loaded the car and got out of the car
I pulled my arm from the seat through the carpeted woods
Dead cars in the culvert, the woods, and the stream
Wind shapes moved off like hands through the reeds

Something small, something toothed, wriggled in mud
At times—still and wakeful—moaning—I watched
A nipple, the pines, blue stones, and then words
Just put up a finger; say something wet

And your face will rise up and shimmer with eyes
I'd never been that close to a shape
It's like trying to say the water is "there"
And flow over rocks and glimmer at once

You pulled your arm from the wall, sticky with shapes
Later—we died—in your room—with our mouths
Light slickened the leaves—the wind—it's not me
Beyond that: a wall, more skeptical trees

FETISHISM

A storm above land, swirled over, unthought
While light filled the fields with tinier eyes
The saints flashed their mirrors, the windows surged up
I go over there—but it doesn't exist

Difficult too was how the things mooed
How milk increased, how the path flew away
The wind fattened itself and fluffed up the leaves
I really don't know which thing could be me

This is where in the story that the "I" turns to "crimes"
The film works like this and it pushes me back
To run along then through blue fields of chalk
The words take their line from the unreadied dead

I discovered dead men and their system of cars
Their smoking system: *How to lie on the grass*
With hair photographed and your face wrinkled up
While the distance resigned or held out a tree

I stared at that cross disguised as a tree
And evolved—of my brain—some more wooden brains
In the mirrors: "pine boughs," "fog," and then "rain"
I should have said "stains": my body was there

PLEASURE HOUSE

This table tastes like old weather was here
I'd approached through the fog, spinning off body heat
And it's like a voice flowed over some beings laid out
In the window: a cloud—it's "the difficult face"

After that I began to have fingers and eyes
And climbing the hill noticed noises on plants
It was then that I sat and looked back on the sea
That was after I'd stared at the coins in my head

I glowed and missed the chambers of court
Where I was expressed in the window and desk
Oh pleasure—I thought—these lips—I'm alive
While Pussycat mewled and slept on its drugs

I think it means I want to go serve
But it's hard to rummage so much in the sea
To slip open each shape, with a slobbery sound
I went over there—but it didn't exist

Oh north boundary—east boundary—shapes in the fog
Knee-high ornamentals—fog stains—on the walls
I'm a short-term, successful sequence of dirt
I've said it before, the sea rips me in half

LIKE THE DIRT
(5 CEREMONIES)

★

when we ran
it was called
     "the fighting"
"with the grass"

on our legs
  the left ones
we placed
the simple words

as if we ran
   on our buttocks
      as if we fell
in large drops

silence
came
   as if feathers
lay dead

*

just for walking
on the tar
like with fingers
    now for stumps

    in the Blinding
Mirrorthing
trees
  are motionless

it's the earth
we'll have to wear
  and smear
  your mirror head

secretly
we ate
    the paintings
of each place

★

ensorcelled
in bark
in gnarled
blue skin

"we grasped
one another
and entered
the dirt"

nothing
but words
much
did they gleam

squares
of white light
   on the floor
of the wind

*

we fed birds
in my dream
in my life
from your hands

at the sign
   of small claws
I have to wear
  this old head

a gesture
a lip
 the shadow
of haste

and then drive
   the burgundy
   cars
in the earth

*

the years
went whirling
    there was shaking
of their capes

dying
  on their backs
is called
"it has a back"

or pressing
       soft   blue
chunks
  to the words

there is going
    by each one
in secret
    like the dirt

MOUTH GUITAR

PRODIGALS

Do the spent later return
because they'd forgotten something? Food?
Beneath the barrel of leaves
they thought the god would drool

or something, to see them
torn from this book.
But must we go on with these Swarms of the Judge
Horsebacked, Bewhipped, Pommelhand-Drawn

and the way they fix me
in gaze with the ranch?
Perhaps I would never—
and the barrel, the fence.

Like when riding in the hills
one tosses back one's head . . .
But now, the night and jasmine unfold
and the land gets promised

to someone at the end.
Meantimes, I, the poet, have returned from nearby
to be far away from you
with you and all my words.

But now you have the words—
with the little pictures they arrive,
to be near you, inside you
just when they disappeared. You'll see here a small deer

in the arms of the erased. Here is the river
where the capture of the deer, and the
forest and the war and the vast
gray poisoned lake. Meanwhile the light is changing,

rolling down the sky
to a lot, behind a fence, with the weeds
and now the stumps. Feathered, prehistoric,
we are drying in their throats

and are echoed, and brought further,
over distance, by the doves.
But will you buy what I have bought,
will you hold it to your zone

and smell it with your lips
while I squeak on you like doves—
"I, in this symphony of god,
am your head, I am drowning your head,"

that's what their song said.
But here our bodies turned away, each burrowed toward
    its core,
and the image that was there and flickered
and went on. Riding back

in the truck, white leaves poured overhead
like song words in light rain
till the strategy devolved
and at dawn we were possessed,

like in the frieze or photograph,
on the patio   and damned
with ornamental froth.
So the god turned us into furniture

in its songs about the past.
You've been squirming for three minutes now
with its words under your flesh,
stuck into your skin, by this radiant quack.

And the cheese on the counter grows wet and more sick,
and the news day is slick
with more thoughtless heat.
But then the birds began in unison:

"why lock up your throats?"
One can start again, there are gestures between thoughts,
a slipping out of pants, and into different dress:
a mustache and a wing—and every Tuesday add a tusk,

or painted goiter on the hip
out by the foam-injected stones.
But then life caught up with us again
and then two years and then the war

beneath the surface of our jobs,
as the light will rise and fall
on the patch of dirt we made,
to which we'd sworn to turn away,

and grow tubers and a school
of congealed light and noise.
Staggering now, with nothing like a will,
we round the corner of that house

and burst onwards towards home.
Then Day, so friendly sometimes, so sometimes
far away, on the hillside with the forehead rocks
and the tiny golden birds, appeared

on all the roadways, on the grass patches
with the shrubs, in the trees
that money placed, next to the on-ramp,
in the swamp. I remember once, under those trees,

while inside our bones grew dark,
cars whooshed and rubber flaked
along the edges, with the light.
It was of the edges the light spoke

and of the shapes preceding names
that flew in patterns through our lungs:
a wren, I thought, *a face*. "Birdbath,"
you said, and straight out of that bush

a hummingbird rose at a speed beyond breath.
Another one born, shrinking, lifted up.
It's all, as the song goes,
too beautiful for votes.

The light gestures again at the longing for delay
as well as the devotion to arrival and change.
But this curtain of forms, California,
is a fetish for all kinds of enforcers

who wield the pulsing blob of lines
by which we are each removed from the earth.
Are persons like ours really needed
to carry these bodies and eyes?

And so back again to the city
and the red flow, from vents,
of the names. Buried under the house
with our umbilical cords and our names

we're alone again in their dream.
This was the meaning of catch and release.
But the very next day charm returned,
as the true source of life as we knew it: charm of the lips,

our charming limbs, a movement of voice
and the lids. So in our caskets
we left rods and sticks
and hid out again in the trees.

It's this need for adventure in everyday life,
to take the wrong turn in the park
and discover the forest they left there
where men suck each other and fuck. That lake

is covered in soundproofing and the hawks here
are smaller and fleet. They jet between pines,
then squawk, and soar out over the ridge and the cars.
I think they have multiple souls, or

I think we have multiple souls.
I see us down there in the gulch
with the streaming light and the mud
when we stared at the birch long enough

to begin to sprout leaves in your blood.
But nighttime's home improvement
draws us out again from the trees
over the lawns, helplessly houseward,

and the neighbors rush inside.
So we vote for more darkness,
tall grass, and more wind: moonrise over the damned.
Let this moment stand for me, myself,

addressed to you, paused in the doorway
at the trauma near the end. The shadow
of my hat falls flat across my face, obscuring
all the features there. And you, in the ski mask

smirking in the hall—what will happen next?
So taking care to wipe the knobs
we padded backwards down the stairs;
the neighborhood had vanished

in the mirrors and the screens. Night beat against our hips
like bodies in a gym. It was as if we could proceed
unarmed into the woods and there
find a bed of furs and feathers in the dirt

and resting there and dreaming
regain our bodies and their limbs
and then emerge along the wires that led back into the mall.
And so we'd see you there, on the corner

at the light, face shadowed by your hoodie,
leaning on the oak, when we passed
in borrowed cars on our way to get more drugs.
Rewind the film, repeat, watch the bellies of the leaves

in slow motion lifted up by speed and then the wind.
First the wind, then the grass, then the words began to tick
and the next thing that I touched was your body on the screen.
But soon a less personal question arose—

that of loneness . . . touching the food . . .
How to explain it to others
in your bathrobe driving west to a sound
or dazed by a jade plant at noon?

The colors are perfect but the lines are unreal
for the dreamless afflicted by road signs and blur.
Still, if over each object at once each of our bodies inclines,
and if the words of description each utters

shake through the bodies and air,
can't we say that the object is singing, that its absence,
like presence, is there? It's like it was in the beginning
in the world back on the farm.

The hungry shapes were willing—the barrels and the boats.
Love in the foreground would trace a twisted bough,
and in the glitter on the ice, that vanishment was yours.
The others gathered there in families

at the edges, at the shore. Is there any hope for us at all,
    they said.
Not for us, they said.
So coming back now from the North,
Life foretold itself again, bloviated, blank,

on top of all of this. Take it with you, please,
like a photo of these chairs
impersoned on the dock
and left there with the years.

MOUTH GUITAR

I

These small gruntings I make while trying to get comfortable—
they churn in the dust like more dust.
But the pillows are finally stacked correctly
so that more rupture can begin. I read:

  "This has been lubricious"

"Throat sap in the trees"

And then closing the book.
My flesh is as dark ramps to your fears and their fleetingness.
You cannot predict these sudden implosions
but touching another, you decide to begin.

So little has drooled through my brains this morning
that I can give you the complete account of it:
Tube notes
awash
in blue glow

Raptures of Hair
in the Machines of the Light

I am here today though my throat is prenatal

And so many words, though they have to be covered with pain
    and ferment
so that rooftops can glow

false
carnivorous   bowling   goes on

I didn't wish to be touched like a face
in the bland topical seemings of that place.
But returned to our seemings it goes on a long time, mouthing
deliberately: you still have to perform them.
And so much severity they have as down the shifting hills
stumble the weathered lips, with the blissed-out face far
    behind them.

Later a small dream climbed up the leather stairs
parallel to the earth and your perception of the house
reappeared in an expression of violent blue lines. That
    presence
with the image in it became considerably more present.

The recognition remains constant
though the bodies and faces have changed
in this moment spared of all hope.

You see yourself there in a girl/boy suit
from when they still made worlds at home
hiding there, in abstract space
while the voices migrate above you.

Something frontier, buckskin and fringed
     The two sides are connected by shock
And Mother, in the middle of gestures
   But you must not do it like that.

2

I returned from the street where I had searched all the bins for
your ticket and receipt. The early light exposed the brutality
of the neighbors, always hacking up the plant life, right there,
where it glows. But I have tried to fold my judgments into my
body where they are transmuted into new sounds, song—and
the comedy of a man my size climbing out of that little car and
discovering once again all the stains on his hat. *I don't think he
was "a good man" or that he should have shot all those people, but
a few more cops would've been fine by me.*

blue world   green world
with sunlight on its hands

I see I am approaching the splendid host, right there
where she lives, on the twig
I ask if she has any more pigments left
whether these feathers on the branches are for guests
and am delighted when she answers, "Yes."

And you, being there near the cold, but not true, presence
Does you hear what I is saying?

Is you is?

(*Neighbor*, I whispered.)

It's a "human moment," dressed up in skins
ankle-tethered to the glowing land—
It rattles and drags, it pauses and leaps.

(*Neighbors*, I whistled.)

But these sodden busts of cement and blood
are so nimbused by the growing density of the seen

whose moment saps them of all characteristics
that we all flicker there, in the stammering name.

Still, after blending and hugs . . . like a filthy mass,
the sky beat above us

booming with space whenever a sound . . .

and only the fear of space prevents us.

Let's move in closer and examine its mouth
and the shapes the sun makes when it enters your mouth.

Mightn't these shapes be sufficient
to represent sadness, the pause in your head,
and the way your coat moves
as it glides out beyond you?

Through that forest of cops in the forest
I couldn't perceive the trees they allowed.
But the leaves tapped at the solid glass block
and Nowhere, or deep, a small phone was heard.

It blinds me with pleasure:
the mouth
  of the Day

Then Space again—
Distance, thickened
with rain

    *

And then one morning, just like a squirrel,
pain arrived suddenly
but much bigger and faster than anyone told me. A blur
of whiskers and panic, it climbs straight up the wheel;
it won't stop even to think.
Why do you want to go there, we all say. But pain goes where
    it is.

A voice on the tape said burn the motherfucker. A voice on
    the tape says
burn him out now

while on the street the little tents shook
with the voice and the motions of the bodies inside.

We made much of that space
where bodies leapt up
and of the distance in everything's lips
where we always found something real
later, to reflect on later, and repeat.

Then the fluid, that turned out to be "the voice" in the
    diagram,
goes through each body and ends at the dump

and a mouth heaps forward the beats in the dirt.

The problem is that it is expectation
that guides these slow thoughts over the plants,
and projects into a finer expression
all the fingers I forgot.

Did that shape just come out of my body?

            There it flickers, unresolved.
Breathing . . . each . . . my toes inflate.

Handing over the money, crossing the street.

    3

Now the pulsing afternoon
takes each belly in its hands
lifts it up towards some glass
and all that's inside

While he crawled on
with his body
towards vengeance
or the state

Later
sweeping up
they shift their curtains
unto dusk

And in that drooling shade
the kids grew older and away

"Neighbors," I whittled, "there is no longer any cultural form
that would allow me to directly address you (perhaps there
never was), but my animate body is (right now) sliding down
a hillside of fragrant herbs, spring flowers, and the usual trash.
I roll and roll on past a sequence of forms, locked into each
other, slurping and hot"

We should begin each day like these word-hands imagined
folded asleep on their bodies and sheets
or reaching up to the window (where sex is asleep)

or in a mammal suit, where we appears on the land
to scuttle, and stand and glare back at the land.

New voices dangled from each of the leaves.

All this awaits us—
touching and mouths,

   wordplay and laughter,

with sex in our mouths.

It just starts again, or it starts to repeat.

But the sex, for all we spoke of it, was no more theoretical
than the lamplight on the leaves and the last
car at the end of the lot—that brittle car was ours.

I could hear the age humming: the industrial age, where it
   ended
in words, in some bodies onstage.
                  But when we pulled back the curtain
the apparatus was there, it hammered and stank,
where we fed it raw hands.

So the hourly scenes
thickly descend

plucked and zoned for mixed use. The feeling drifts
of being you
through shoulders to the trunk.

And you return to the surface
again and again
consulting the funerals there

 "ribbons are flung, ribbons of cloud"

        hillside
numerals burn

in a sequence of bald disaffection
though the music is lovely, and real.

THIS LIVING HAND

All this rancor, you said, towards your poem.
Words have better things to do than count on us
to see them, they know when we aren't there.
And I bet the reader might regret
touching these lips, where weather insists
in a smatter of life and blue shapes.
Maybe we'll disappear instead.
No memories rushed in to replace you:
it's been almost eight years
in a haze of creatured shapes.
Stepping through doors isn't the whole of it
though that's the part that stands out—
porch lingering, hands to the lips
with more confusions on the stairs.
We should all get back to the bus.
But then I reached the curb and thought
this is a poem *about* something
forgotten, or misdreamed;
the tire stank, went flat
in that dirt, miles from home.
"Border towns," I thought, "it's the musics
that I miss. The way
some people talked, or didn't talk

and stared. Then at night, when it's warm
the little wizards all came out
to take off their real hats
and ask me how you've been."
In the plaza thoughts were singing . . .
the rooftops smeared with rain.
Gentle reader, I remember,
I see you there like that
forgotten on the bench
underneath the paper mask.
The clatter of the rain
resembled small machines
that imitate the hands
smacking masa into shapes.
After that I felt expensive,
or fragile, overpriced. The ironwork gleamed,
the stone gutters slurped.
The sky came no nearer, and then closer again
as our bodies were taken
like dreams through the weeks
and dropped at the gates
with a stub and receipt.
I believe that it's happened,
somewhere we've arrived
on wet stairs once again
staring up at the words.

But now the music is sick,
the planet is sick, the mud
vomits bones, buttons,
and wings. It's all about
Fluctuation, this riding
on whips, greater than self
ripping holes in the dirt.
This much the hand described
before it turned too diaphanous,
too dispersed in what it touched
to be seen among the shapes
that the present tense allowed
there behind the chutes.
So that later when that species
staggers off to sleep,
we still won't know what it was like
to make behaviors or to think.
This tube leads to your mouth,
and through your mouth to pain
and beyond the pain to place:
a plate of light under the waves.
So the feeling builds—
a dread, as of events.
It's part of us, the real part,
this being there, unwed.
A bird passes in the window

is reflected in the case . . .
And the things all weep with presence,
which passes
     as the light
         brushes every surface
like the master'd
touched your face.
Like you'd said we were all there
where his thoughtless penis dripped.

And death   and rainy posters
on the walls
that led out back.

Now I should imagine
with my body if possible
this handle that your anger has.
Yes, this is a treasure
and I must never touch it—
but oh to *be* it
here, here, and here.
You see, the government
still controls everything,
or nothing, which is to say: location.
It's in charge of all that
though neither it nor

it "exists"
biologically speaking. Though
sometimes inside the structures
a thumping, perhaps recorded,
as of life is heard,
of organs, and possibility,
which therefore exists
as green and translucent as this hand.
A hand from nowhere. A hand
with nowhere to stand, twitching like weather
across the business sheets.
This is what it is to believe
and to eat and then arrive
in a structure through hard work
and self-deceit. The role
of portraiture and the
police in all this is clear
but what, you may ask,
do love and friendship entail
growing roots
through all your speech
so it's like someone exists?
This is time
leaking through silt,
green light on the leaves,
the invisible beats.

Here at Pleasureland
this is how it works. A poem
leads out
as quiet as your hand,
Daylight's first expression
that everything forgets.
Eyes rolling out of tune
with the morning
of the year,
but it's true if you look:
we are lucky at this.
And the shyness overcame
the holy treason of the lips
and forces us to be
in the grasses with the wind.
We put an asterisk
down that tallest slope
and eagerly—the stones,
a ribbon of notes.
Each moment of the transition,
once it had passed,
brought the stranger back
to love in your arms. Pet it now
there where it lives,
where it purrs and talks,
where it eats.

At night it sings of departure
and wind, but in the morning
it's there as nude as your limbs,
opening its pinkish mouth,
under the glowing sky.
You sit there together
with day's blue on your fur,
like the distance on snow,
on the mountains and roads.

Knuckle flesh

     tongue trace

          a shoulder blade
       a spine.

And the neck beneath the hair,
plunging to the brain.

Meanwhile the tall grass
moves like an animal, like the wind

in the hairs of an animal, as we move quickly,
over the land, to a view

of more distance, where all the bees touch,
and the smell of sage rises
like food or like hands. I follow
the sense differently now; I follow you now,

you are speaking again. Through hallowed slits
your voice illuminates these wigs
where the scribes, in grassy light,
touch the power of the wind.

Let me touch your head, shouldn't it be real,
shouldn't it be red, the light now
at the ridge, where it travels
through the lizards and the slits

between their heads? It all seems
anachronistic, the desert
and the sea, the mountains
and the monks, *California-by-the-Land*.

The dirigible sun, while you glanced away,
stamped the further wall,
stripping it of names. Meanwhile
we're unhappy, cumbersome, and mean.

What is it with people, all struggling
to mean? Many still are fooled;
they think they're near
or far away. And later, they come in, to contribute

to the meal, with the stories of their feats,
the witty things they did, or imagined
that they'd said—Loquacious Hammering—
while you stir the mint into the beans

and think of sex unfolding limbs. Meanwhile lumps
are coming back, in the viewer
and the land. Shadows shift across the dunes,
tracks stammer in the sand, crossing at the crests

where the flowers wiggle up
and shimmy in the wind that pauses and moves on.
The creatures lift their ears, sand rushes
in the holes, and in the photos of the holes

in the *Guide to Desert Holes*. Addressed
to itself, the weather cannot fail.
More bodies step forward,
it seems, or are still, the lips

slightly moving, like lizards
through hair. He's probably one of us, we think;
we think she might be real
like a Viking, or a Slave,

more bodies on the way. 1,000 years
from Vikings to this page:
warmongers, babies,
axes through the brains—

I have never seen it. But once, visiting
on the plains above the sea,
I heard the ancient tongue
in the mouth of a school bird

walking past me with a fiend
toward the schoolhouse and the end.
There is no end to it,
just more bellies packed with ice

and more weather, and more lips
all asking you to groan
where an I feels famine
in the humps under the toads.

It's then your hand appeared
and flickers in the hut
near your sandy head
and the sequins on the screen

that rustled like the dust
or scales of something real.
It's a method, I thought—
"Performance," you croaked—

where we pray on the ground,
to nibble at our hands, root in the coals,
and get ash on our heads,
then rest, unperturbed, under the oaks.

I'm not here, it means,
or here, or here, or here. It's there
where I am not, or have already been
as the shadows lick the meats, the desk

legs, and the strings. It's time to close the station
and watch the money slip away.
Your fingers pressed into my skin,
leaving whispers,

little names, while night
prowled along the shoulders
of the handles and the chairs.
There's nothing like you in the world

while I was pouring in your ear
right there, at last, nightly
parking in that burg.
Then my body soldiered on,

over swaying hills, to the solitary tree
where I found you once again
leaning on a stone and
smirking with your head—

"sexually," said the script,
which instructs the crystal thing
like the river of canoes
that glides through swaying reeds.

And then we flow down all those grooves
and went back into the rooms
where the bodies get invisible,
and are objects of a quest.

Meanwhile in the cities,
the armored goons of state
have closed up all the cities and demanded,
with success, that the little people hide

or sweetly not exist,
so the manhunts can continue, for ones
with halves, and flanks—
meaty ones, the doomed

crouching in the boats.
Lean in to smell this leather,
there are people traces here
and the lumber, and the rust

of afternoon—the bank,
dull afternoon, the street,
its glare, and principles,
tea, cash, and self-possession,

the cars, and window glass.
Water is crushed,
squeezed down through the cracks.
Personality roared

back down the line
and on the other street
I saw the shards and plastic heads,
ears, doll parts, the hair,

and little hands. I photographed this world
and sent it to your phone.
It is, I said, an image
of a barrel and a twig, standing

like a chin, in aisle seven
near the bread. There I wonder at your hat,
the grass, the drying grass
and the small blue flowers

in the grey and purple dust. And then the sun explodes,
became an act we stayed behind
beside the little car
that someone must have smoked.

And when they see us, they'll see birds.
And then we're backing up
like bluster in the trees
and beeping, like the months.

THE SELECTED

SUSURRATIONS

this is it
some kind of
voice
thread to pull
you out
across   the shining
plates
through
the window   illusion

      of distance
             fields
a few
trees
  tossed
fat with wind
in the

feathered grass
a girl
nurses
a wolf
it's famous

                    tiny
people

the world
is a
yammering ghost
say the dead

the world
is wind
in a cup

THE DAY
(PAPER BOAT)

In the mirror
when you lift your hands
in my hands
I cup the light.
The world
is smeared
with hands.
I bring it
to my lip.
little leaf
      my paper boat
The world
is smeared
with lips.
When there
you taste your salt
      right
      here
I taste
my salt.
The light drooling

on your hip
is pooling
on my hip.
Teeth
are living teeth,
bones
are silver bones.
Grass
and tree
are motionless.
Did you see
the pulsing doves
when I see
the brutal doves?
        Time
          swirled up
in Flocks.
little leaf
        my paper boat
Day crawled
across the grass.
Your fingers
touched my back.
I learned
about the grass.

POEM

As if this place weren't also a location,
this chair—arrived at—my destination:
this moment through my skin.
Attention rides in pulses—
electric worm—or skipping stone—
now from my ankle to my toes
and I *am* the floor and then I'm toes
touching the floor and never

        the two at once.
And then the presence
of my curling uncut nails
(cut my nails, on my
things-to-do, after
shopping, food and texting you)
is interposed, a third term called
the world between—I mean—
I cannot feel my nails
but rather the gap they make
between my toes and floor
as this kind of urgent void—
a pressure where I am today.
This weather thinks of you.

AMTRAK
ON HUDSON

I pushed
my body through

all this
 speed

to you

 texting

The Surface

Light
goes
 pouring through

It's
my wrist

Invisible
Thumb

the tip
of this tongue

is a bright

Intestinal

Moment

gone to link

  the tip
with the Lake
of Meat

one
  bright
   hair
from there

to the city

straightened out
 dreaming
or in flight

The lip
of the tongue
is touch

leaving marks

gently
to the silk

riding
on the train

the river

and the birds—

 Leaves moved
on that table

like bellies
in the wind

 I was made
for this pleasure

my nose
against the THING

    Or lifting up
a single egg
to contemplate
that egg

  Or rub that egg
on both my wrists
and dissolve
my living head

It's that train
we say
 "is gone"

to faces
in green rooms

of telephones
and breaths:

the Mothers
in a field

VOW

Friendship and love are in my blood
they are there for you,
Dear Lady.
But if I say this blood for real,
if I take it out
show it   name
it   there is no way
to expose
yet not expose it.
I mean I didn't mean
to take it out.
But how I gather when I think of you,
how I gather *there*
in this pleasing pressing urgency.
It insists itself a substance.   Look.
Will you look
at it
It is there
It is mute   it is
greedy will you
touch
it
It is all

addressed to thee   It is

the most

universal non

universal

strangest

thing about me?

It is not

Mine it is

Yours? It is

more *Me*

than mine. It is

not. I don't know

where it came from but

I remember.

I am hairy now

as I have been

down all my body

to the zone. My blood

is full of sparks,

Dear Lady. They are not sparks.

I cannot speak today.

LITTLE BODIES

I am taken
to the moment world
Here when I am named
I am named my favorite name
In your poem I am "you"
I just knew it would be you
I knew there would be palms
open-handed trees and
your head upon the sky
The rocks upon the sky
The sky upon the sky
where the mountain pours its noise
on the real bodies there
assembled there like rocks
the rocks that bleed in poems
I feel also there's a horse
And I think this horse is real
This horse is thinking eyes
while the rocks keep bleeding light
But I don't want justice
All I want is love
I said I don't want justice
I said all I want is love

Love listens to a horse
It listens to a tree
And here there is a horse
And this happens to a tree
to the little bodies everywhere
gone lurching in your poem
Love listens with your eyes
to these bodies on the ground
The little bodies in your eyes
go streaming on the ground

BANK HOLIDAY

The gray mouth
of the sky
lowered softly
over the parking lots
and the buildings
and the revelers slept
crumpled as sheets
behind the black screens
of computers
that sat on
pasteboard furniture
littered with heartbreaking notes
because in the poem
like the photograph
like the movie
everyone is already dead
our beautiful bodies
recomposed
of another substance
the one you touch here
in the poem
real skin   inhuman
hair   an eerie

absence of
bird sounds
I was sleeping
on *these* clouds
water and hair
and light
poured over my body
and then I woke
    you were sleeping
but out there
beyond the poem
we'd been dead
for years   everything
we didn't know
that happened happened there:
the years puffed out
with days and blood
on skin beneath
the artificial lamps
But today
in my poem
there's just a bus
It's a real bus—
The Bus Forever
It is empty
as today is empty

empty as a dream
a holiday today
in a city
where we walk
with real hands
clasped
in imagination
As the dream flows
words to pictures
empty
buses bloom
in poems   flowers
are soaked
with tiny beasts
their little bodies
wet with hair
and still
in my poem
in my bed
you are sleeping
in the part of you
I will never touch
no matter how far
I'd put my fingers
up   reaching there
to brush the bone

the word *Flesh*
the word
Drink
the words
Wet   and
Gone

THE SELECTED

I want a brighter word than bright
with a glimpse of sea
that I may feel
I am at a pleasant window
have seen your comet
and kissed your writing over
in the hope
you had indulged me with a trace
For in a city of melancholy men
all made so by circumstance
I am given to bode ill
But I took your letter to bed with me last night
In the morning I found your name
descending to the earth like a magic basket
The certainty you are in the same world as myself
Oh It could effect a cure

★

Here they hunt the picturesque like beagles

They raven down scenery

like children do sweetmeats

But all day I have been employed in a most abstract poem

I see you through a mist

As I dare say you see me

My mind is stuffed like a cricket ball

My forehead is on the ground

I beg your pardon for it

(Oh if through me my

illness may have touched you!)

But you have ravished me away

I have seen you

★

On the night I was taken

by a rush of blood

beyond the doors and windows

Lips! Why talk about such things

I hold the dearest pleasures in the universe

I have a consolation independent of them in the certainty

    of your affection

I shall kiss your name

and mine (where your lips have been)

Why talk about such things   Lips!

This world I believe is both singular and plural

You are a thousand

I shall kiss your name

*

I am melting for the fire
Day by day I am not deceived
My mind was ever put
into a body in the room
I get use of my chest
I linger on the borders
I fly out of the window
I am much better this morning
I shall not suffer
like glass breathed upon
but be always bright
The fire will annul me

★

What a horrid climate
What careless inhabitants it has
There's the thrush again—
How can you bear so long an imprisonment
I could build an altar to you for it
but I cannot be easy
At some future time I propose
to forego future time
and all likely circumstance
But you understand the whole matter
Do not step or move an eyelid
Please think of me all day

*

I am greedy of you
going to town alone
but I have seen you the whole time
A vision: How I ached
Please fill me with names
enough to occupy the widest heart
Then I see you again
at a greater distance
I see life bedewed in faces
May you exclaim, tantalized
as other men and women do
I am greedy of you
But I see life   Good bye

★

Loose a favorite bird
Confess if your heart is too much
too much fastened on the world
There are cruel things beside you!
I feel the effect of hours in my side
I am an object intensely in a room
I am not the same as you
You have a thousand activities
You can be happy and savage
I breathe in a room You
breathe in a room
The sun rises and sets
The sun rises and sets
Feeling passes
Everything tastes like my mouth

★

It would have pained me to have seen my own head
If I am the Theme I will not be the Friend
But every hour I am more concentrated in you
Everything else tastes like my mouth
My mouth tastes like years and the years taste like brass
Suppose me in a magic glass
I am glad there is such a thing

ACKNOWLEDGMENTS: This book is traversed by the work of too many poets to list here. I will have to content myself with naming those two poets whose presences in the book are most insistently diurnal. The poem "The Selected" is composed entirely of words, often entire phrases, from the letters of John Keats. Elsewhere in the book Keats' famous fragment "This Living Hand" provides the title of one poem, and pops up in several. The third section of this book emerged from a long period spent particularly companioned by the richly companionate work of John Ashbery. Of special importance to the poems in that section were his books *Hotel Lautréamont* and *Rivers and Mountains*. Appropriated, re-worked, misheard, and otherwise distorted language from these books and others is scattered through the three poems in that section. In addition to these two poets, I thank all the poets and writers living and dead, all the friends and family, and all the forgotten strangers who traverse both myself and this book. I thank the following people whose thoughts on these poems were crucial to their emergence: Kirsty Singer, Joshua Beckman, Matthew Zapruder, Matthew Rohrer, Noelle Kocot, and Mark Allen. I thank the editors of the following publications where some of these poems first appeared: *MAKE*; *BOMBlog*; *Poor Claudia*; *A Public Space*; *Ghost Town*; *Spoke Too Soon*; *Forklift, Ohio*; *textsound*; *Jupiter 88*. I also wish to thank Machine Project, the Poetic Research Bureau, and KChung: these community sites nurtured this book as it grew. Thanks also to Karen McCann and our walks on the Punsit Road. The poem "The City" is dedicated to Occupy LA. "Like the Dirt" is for CAConrad and Kevin McCann. This book is dedicated to Kirsty Singer.